TULIPMANIA

TULIPMANIA
The Skagit Valley Tulip Festival

Official Festival Guidebook

Stephen Herold

photography by
Steve Westman

CELESTIAL ARTS

ACKNOWLEDGMENTS

I would like to offer my thanks to several people who worked hard to make this book happen. First, in effort and importance, is Rachel Wyman of Burlington, WA. Her research and collection of materials saved months of work. The encouragement of Jim Turk and Audrey Medved of the Festival office was much appreciated. Margaret Lee offered information, assistance and good coffee.

The Monet quotation is from: Monet: A Retrospective, *ed. Charles F. Stuckey, Park Lane, 1986. The information originally came from an interview the Duc de Trévise had with Monet in 1920 as printed in* La Revue de l'Art Ancien Et Moderne *in Jan-Feb 1927.*

All photographs except the following are by Steve Westman:
Stephen Herold—3,4 (two at bottom left), 31, 46, 48 (upper right), 59 (top), 63 (left center)
Lynn Hollaman—23, 39 (top), 45, 53 (bottom), 59 (bottom), 62 (bottom), 67
Galen Larson—32

Book and cover design by Stephen Herold
Cover Painting by Don Smith
Typography by Lasergraphics
Printing by Northwest Graphics

Celestial Arts
P.O. Box 7327
Berkeley, California 94707

First Printing 1989

Manufactured in the United States of America

ISBN: 0–89087–584–7

*This book is dedicated to
Buster Lee, Ed Dalan and, especially, Max Clark.
They had a magical touch with growing plants and an eye
for all that was essential.*

INTRODUCTION

*T*O A BIRD flying overhead, the Skagit delta is a picture book triangle of lush farmland edged by hills and mountains. Except for a few wooded hills and watercourses, it is entirely covered with a patchwork of farms and their neat rectangular fields. The colors change with the seasons; from winter's subdued browns and grays to the fresh green of spring, rich gold of summer and back to the fresh brown earth of fall plowing.

In the spring the green is interspersed with immense blocks of brilliant color. The roads are lined by hundreds of acres of yellow mustard and cabbage, the Skagit Valley being one of the world's main sources of their seed. But most spectacular of all are the fields of blossoming bulbs—daffodils, tulips and irises. More are grown here than anywhere else in the world. The scale of the growing is also grand, with some bulb fields running to over 100 acres. As spectacular as home gardens can be, it is hard to imagine the impact of hundreds of acres of tulips.

Although we may find such fields delightful to look at during an afternoon's drive from the city, they are not there as decoration or entertainment. The Skagit Valley is a serious farming area and the bulbs are raised as a profitable crop. The bonus for us is that they bloom and we get to enjoy them. The farmers of these bulbs are also good businessmen and promoters. With the same pride of rural America that created the Gilroy Garlic Festival and the Watsonville Artichoke Festival in California, they began the Tulip Festival in Skagit County's Mount Vernon

This book is an introduction to the Tulip Festival, and a brief guide to the lower Skagit Valley. No attempt has been made to offer a complete guide to everything you may find or need in the valley. There is always some new and unexpected delight in the Skagit Valley, and you will find your own.

The 1892 Tillinghast seed catalog. All of the early catalogs had similar covers. Much of the printed material used at the seed company was produced on the small clamshell letterpress that is still on display there. I printed seed packets on it as late as 1978.

TABLE OF CONTENTS

Chapter 1
GEOGRAPHY & SETTLEMENT

*L*IKE ALL OF WESTERN WASHINGTON, the Skagit Valley was shaped by the influence of glaciers and rushing water on a young volcanic landscape. There were other mountains and valleys here on the edge of the North American continent. Long since worn down to hills, they survive as in the Willapa Hills south of Olympia. In the last few million years, the Americas have collided with the Pacific plates of the earth's crust, thrusting up vast volcanic mountains from Alaska to Patagonia. Some started as offshore islands that were scooped up and joined to the mainland, like the Olympic Mountains. The main ranges, running north to south, are cut by drainage valleys where the storm waters run back to the sea.

The Skagit Valley has been most fortunate in its setting, the west coast being significantly milder than the east owing to the prevailing west to east winds. Western Washington is in the same latitudes as Newfoundland and central Siberia yet has nothing of their severe climate. The high Cascade-Coast ranges, stretching in an unbroken arc from western Alaska down the Americas, protect Puget Sound from Arctic air in winter (*usually*—1989 has been a notable exception). The Olympic Mountains protect it from ocean storms, and the mighty Skagit River has cut the valley while bringing rich volcanic silt and moisture to make it so fertile. Despite the fact that the Skagit river is only 100 miles or so long, in the western U.S. only the Columbia and Sacramento rivers carry a greater volume of water. No one who has seen the Skagit in full flood would doubt it.

Thousands of years ago, as the glaciers melted, the land gradually rose as it was freed from their immense weight. This exposed the shallows of Puget Sound, which filled with silt to form some of the finest farmland in the world. As the Skagit River played and cut its way back and forth across a wide delta, it lay down deep beds of rich clay, often four or five feet deep. The valley's aquatic origins are not entirely gone, however. At high tide salt water flows under large areas of the valley through its underlying sands, and the lower valley literally floats on the sea. Were it not for the dikes that hold the sea and river back much of the valley would also be under water at high tide, or during floods. It is not greatly different from Holland which, interestingly enough, brings our thoughts to tulips, as it did to others long ago.

The twisting streams of the Skagit Delta water a tideland rich in marine life. This is one of the few natural tidal areas left in Skagit County.

As the glaciers retreated life slowly returned to Puget Sound, climaxing in towering evergreen forests. Although forest wildlife was limited owing to the great density of the woods, the shores and waters were rich with marine life. This included the five varieties of Pacific salmon who were the attraction and sustenance of the earliest settlers here. The Coast Indians built a complex and highly sucessful civilization from Alaska to northern California based on fishing, whaling and the gathering of foodstuffs from the hinterland. The immense quantities of fish that could be dried and preserved allowed them much leisure for intricate arts and ceremonies, as well as inter-tribal warfare. With its many watercourses, the Skagit Delta was the seasonal home to local tribes during fishing season. In my garden at the Skagit's mouth I would frequently unearth ancient artifacts and tools; an adjacent archaeological dig found evidence of settlement going back thousands of years.

The first white men came seeking furs, but soon others came to claim and clear farmland as well. It was then that direct conflict began with the Indian way of life that was to so decisively destroy their civilization of thousands of years. Skagit County was settled late, with the first white men coming in the 1850s and 60s. The earliest farmers included Alexander R. Underwood, who built a cabin on Sullivan's Slough at the mouth of the Skagit in 1864, Michael Sullivan and Samuel Calhoun. They began diking the marshlands as these were easier to clear and farm than the dense forests further inland. Alonzo Lowe opened a trading post at what is now La Conner which he sold to John and Louisa Conner in 1869. La Conner took its name from Louisa who, as post-mistress, received mail addressed to L.A. Conner. The name stuck.

1892 fishing cabin at Fishtown. These cabins began on float rafts and were hauled ashore 50 years ago. This is how the Skagit marshes must have looked to the first settlers.

Setlers slowly began moving out to the tangled delta itself. One of the first was Joseph Sharfenberg, who began by thinking the Beaver Marsh area was useless. After some diking and draining, however, he set a number of Chinese laborers to work clearing the land. It took years, but he reclaimed one of the finest and richest farm and bulb areas in the world, with top soil several feet deep. Beaver Marsh Road is the very heart of the bulb fields today, and the Roozengaarde display gardens are located there.

Mount Vernon, the last site in our tulip saga, saw its first settler in the 1870s as Jasper Gates homesteaded what is now downtown Mount Vernon. Not much happened until a major log jam that blocked the river some miles downstream at the tip of Fir Island was removed. Then Mount Vernon became the head of navigation for the river steamers and a hot spot for trade and settlement. Harrison Clothier and Ed English laid out a town on the site and, in 1877, named it for George Washington's home. Many other settlement boom towns thrived and then disappeared, like Skagit City at the site of the old log jam, but Mount Vernon grew and prospered and is now the county seat and largest town in Skagit County.

Early settlements were on the water where transportation was easier than in the tangled forests inland. La Conner was one of the first, and it still is a center for boating, fishing and trade.

La Conner's well preserved buildings and its turn of the century air make it a landmark of Northwest preservation. The famous Gaches Mansion is in the upper right of this picture. In the upper left the large white building is the Garden Club where an earlier tulip festival was held after the Second World War.

Many interesting crafts and antiques can be found in La Conner shops. *(Photos by SH)*

The historic Gaches Mansion in La Conner. It was built by the most successful of a group of English immigrants who came over in the 1880s. It has been extensively restored after a severe fire several years ago and is now used for public functions. It also houses a museum of Northwest art with many fine works by Skagit Valley artists.

Tulip fields on the flats between La Conner and Mount Vernon. The deep clay soil grows large and healthy bulbs.

The settlers in these towns came to Skagit County from all over, but mostly from other northern states and northern Europe. New England, New York, Ohio, Indiana, Illinois, Iowa, Wisconsin, Minnesota, Canada, England, Ireland, Wales, Germany, Luxembourg, Sweden, Norway, Denmark and Finland are all represented. Later settlers included Yugoslavian fishermen, and North Carolinans who helped build the Skagit dams. To many it was a comfortable spot that reminded them of home, but unsettled and open for opportunity. They came to fish, farm, log and enter commerce.

Some were part of group migrations, as with several families that came from the same village in East Anglia in England and settled in and around La Conner. Their names are left as landmarks on the countryside, including Gages Point, Valentine Road and the famous Gaches mansion. It was, of course, more comforting to settle in a strange land with friends and neighbors from home. Finn Settlement was an isolationist colony of Finns. Harmony, next to the famous Beaver Marsh, was a cluster of Swedish farmers. There were even utopian colonies with their (then) radical political or social values. Equality Colony on the north slopes of Bow Hill was a notable example.

Within a few years the rich farm land made the hard working farmers comfortably well off. Many then built elaborate houses like this one to proudly show off their success. Today the houses are all too often abandoned and falling to ruin.

The raising of seed and nursery stock began with one of the early farmers—A.G. Tillinghast. Opening his business in 1885 in the north of the valley near Padilla Bay, he raised and sold seed in a no-nonsense fashion. The company survives today as the Tillinghast Seed Company in La Conner, where he moved it in 1890 when Padilla declined as a commercial site. The family ran it until some ten years ago in a manner little changed over the century of its existence. In his first price list A.G. Tillinghast wrote:

> You can get plenty, nicer and larger catalogues free by applying to the city seedmen. The fancy catalogs are very pretty, but if you want good gardens you must have good seeds. Knowing that you want none but the best seeds, I send you my list of genuine, fresh and reliable seeds. In this list I offer the very best seeds to be obtained. I have chosen only those kinds that I have found to be the best for this climate. Such seeds that I cannot well grow here myself, and those kinds that are better for being grown elsewhere, I have obtained from the eastern and foreign growers. My prices are about one-half what you have to pay for the unreliable store commission seeds. I have made it as easy as I can for you to get my seeds.

This was its philosophy throughout the years the Tillinghasts operated the seed company. I remember Ed Dalen working long and hard to see how inexpensively he could sell his seeds and plants and still pay his bills. People trusted them, and generation after generation of loyal customers ordered stock they knew would do well in the Northwest. You can still shop there today in a slightly modernized and tourist version of the company. The buildings and stock are the same, however, and it is still worth a visit for guaranteed Northwest-compatible seeds and plants.

The importance of Tillinghast on gardens and horticulture in the lower valley can not be underestimated. Many times I was able to identify otherwise unknown old roses or fruit trees by consulting Tillinghast catalogues contemporary with their estimated planting dates. Scarcely an old garden can be found in the Skagit Valley without something from the nursery. The thriving of Tillinghast's business, and the impetus he gave to flowers as well as food crops, were signs of what could be done on such fertile soil. In my 16-page 1892 catalogue, amid the mangel wurzel beets, cabbage, celery, peas, salsify, tobacco and turnips, there is a whole page given to flowers. At the bottom of the page it says:

"☞DON'T forget to select some of these Flowers."

Tulip fields in full bloom in the damp and misty spring of 1988. The soft Skagit air accentuates the brilliant colors of the fields.

Chapter 2
ORIGINS OF SKAGIT BULB GROWING

A S THE POPULATION of Puget Sound rose and life became more settled, the desire for information on the agricultural possibilities of the area led to much experimentation. A Capt. George Gibbs was the first known grower of bulbs in Puget Sound. At his home on Orcas Island he experimented with fruits and hazelnuts; when he had satisfied his curiosity on those plants, by accident he turned to hyacinths. Around 1892 some hyacinths had been injured in planting, and when taken up in the fall were observed to have numerous bulblets attached—a normal way to induce bulb multiplication. These were planted and so a stock in trade resulted. Over the years Capt. Gibbs supplied bulbs to many of the gardens of Whatcom County pioneers.

Gibbs was so proud of his bulbs that he wrote to Dutch bulb growers describing his crop with great enthusiasm and asking for advice. The Dutch were the acknowledged experts in bulbs at the time (and still are in the public imagination) but they responded most unkindly to this wilderness upstart. Not to be denied, Gibbs sent them some sample bulbs. *That* got attention, and shortly thereafter a representative of the Dutch bulb industry visited to see this place that could grow bulbs equal to any from Holland. Not much happened immediately, but the Dutch did not forget Puget Sound.

To assist American farmers, the Department of Agriculture set up three experimental stations for crop research. One was in Whatcom County near Bellingham, which was started in 1907. Dr. David Griffiths was the first director, coming out from Washington D.C.every year for two months in spring and two at the end of summer. It must have been quite a commute in 1907. He soon began growing bulbs to assist the fledgling industry begun by Capt. Gibbs. In fact, the station became the bulb farm of the Bureau of Plant

9

Industry, Soils and Agricultural Engineering. It remained until 1936 when the farm changed to growing trees, and later grasses and legumes. Evidently the bulb industry was felt to be sufficiently established to no longer require government assistance.

Hyacinths and grape hyacinths—Capt. Gibbs' first type of bulbs.

Dr. Griffiths gave some bulbs to Mrs. Mary Stewart, who had recently moved to Samish Island from Ohio and wanted to try raising tulips as her mother had back home. The tulips did well and Mary Stewart ordered some more bulbs from Holland. She reported that she caused great consternation when she asked her bank to cable Holland for the bulbs. This was an unheard of thing to do. When the bulbs finaly arrived half the town turned out to see this foreign oddity. The venture prospered and soon her 40 acres was given over to bulb raising. This gift and encouragement of Dr. Griffiths was to be the origin of Skagit Valley bulb growing, and of today's festival as well.

There was also considerable bulb raising around Bellingham, where some 500 acres were planted in bulbs. In 1920, Bellingham began a Tulip festival that was to last until the Depression made such activities too expensive to maintain. In its heyday Bellingham was known as the Tulip City, and people came from all over the Canadian and American Northwest for the festival.

Special excursion trains and boats brought thousands of visitors each year. Tulips were big business in Bellingham.

Ultimately most of the bulbs were grown east of Bellingham, near Lynden in the Nooksak Valley where there was a large Dutch settlement. These settlers were already familiar with bulbs and quickly took to growing them. Their bulb growing was encouraged by problems the First World War created for importing Dutch bulbs. Even more helpful was an embargo on the import of foreign bulbs in 1926. With the ban many Dutch growers sent

Tulip festival pin from the 7th Bellingham Tulip Festival.

family members to the area to begin bulb farms. The climate around Lynden was too severe for consistent survival of bulbs, however. The fierce northeasters off the mountains could wipe out an entire crop. In 1930 the ban on bulb imports was lifted, which, with the cold weather and the Depression, made the Lynden farms unprofitable.

None of this bothered Mary Stewart since her Samish Island site was thriving—so much that in 1930 she moved her farm to the Skagit Valley. There she found more room and ideal growing conditions for bulbs. With the help of her son Sam, her Tulip Grange Bulb Farm prospered and kept growing. Local farmers, unfamiliar with bulbs, thought this a waste of fine land that could grow such good oats and hay and upbraided her for raising usless triffles. If they had known how profitable bulbs could be they would have changed their tune in a hurry. I know of farmers who are happy to turn a net profit of $50 per acre. Back in 1943, bulbs could turn $250-275 per acre, which would be many times that in today's inflated dollars.

Bulb pickers in tulip fields near La Conner.

One of the most impressive sight is the rippling rows of tulips that change color in broad stripes across the countryside. It is hard to convey the impression of hundreds of acres of flowers in a picture.

Tulips retain their elegant richness even when close up. Here a red and yellow Rembrandt jumps out of a row of less spectacular reds.

In the moist Northwest air a bunch of tulips can be the brightest spot in the landscape.

Each variety is uniquely different, an often overlooked point when viewing vast fields of flowers. As can be seen from the views down into tulip cups, a different viewpoint often shows us new ways of appreciation.

Above: tulips as we commonly see them; upper left: double pink; left center: double yellow; left: red emperor—the first to bloom.

As you move back from the individual flowers, the scope of your appreciation changes. To the left is a medium distance view of peppermint candy tulips; below is a distant view of changing fields of yellow, red, pink and white tulips.

The success of Tulip Grange was not lost on the Lynden farmers, and soon the Stewarts were joined by several Dutch growers who found the answer to their needs in the rich Skagit Valley. There is a story that the Skagit Valley was originally recommended as the superior site for the Bellingham Experimental Bulb Farm after a test growing on the H.L. Willis farm, but that political manuevering brought it to more populous Bellingham.

Now that bulb farming was finally in the Skagit Valley it grew rapidly. By 1940 acreage in bulbs had risen from 30 to 175 acres, and with the Second World War another stoppage of imports boosted demand. The food needs of the war effort prevented taking full advantage of the situation, but bulb growing continued to boom after the war. Many new growers emigrated to the Skagit Valley from Holland after the Second World War. William Roosen, whose Washington Bulb Company is now the largest commercial grower in the United States, was the most noteworthy. Starting as a hired employee for other growers, he gradually built his own business to where the company now has over 2,000 acres of bulbs.

Every business has its specialized side and bulb growing is no exception. There are many market niches for bulbs and the Skagit growers only supplied some of them in the early years. Mary Stewart originally sold largely to garden clubs by mail order, many of them in New England. Later, most of the bulbs were sold wholesale to greenhouse operators for forcing into early bloom for the florist trade. Some greenhouses bought over one million bulbs! Bulbs were also sent back to Holland to be resold to Americans as "Dutch Bulbs". There is a story told by Brian Scheuch of Tillinghast Seed Company about a local woman. She tried to buy bulbs in Holland during the annual tulip festival there, but was told that she couldn't as the bulbs had not yet arrived from the Skagit Valley. Today most of the bulbs are sold to jobbers who broker the bulbs to retail outlets.

In the early days of bulb growing, cut flowers were not sold in any numbers. Lack of refrigeration, slow shipping and lack of an established market were strong deterrents. The greenhouse growers who bought many of the Skagit bulbs were the source of most cut flowers, as they could grow adjacent to their markets and so avoid shipping. It was the large daffodil growers around Puyallup, 100 miles further south, that first began selling cut flowers. Following a suggestion from mayor George Lawler of Tacoma, cut flowers began to be sold in the late 1940s. In the Skagit Valley, H.L. Willis had allowed local Camp Fire Girls to pick and sell some of his flowers previous to this, but no commercial venture followed. It was largely to counter Puyallap that the cut flower trade developed in the Skagit Valley.

Now special plantings are made for cut flowers, and bulbs for sale are deflowered to prevent seed ripening. The growth of air freight has been a great help to cut flower sales; they now are some 25% of total sales.

It is not only tulips that are grown in the Skagit Valley. The fields are a mix between daffodils, tulips, irises and lilies. Interestingly, hyacinths, which were the first bulbs raised by Capt. Gibbs, are hardly grown in the valley now nor are crocuses. Tulips are the most common, followed by daffodils, irises and, least of all, lilies. These all flower at different times and we can enjoy a long season of bloom with repeat visits throughout the spring. The Tulip Festival is only the beginning of the delights of flower raising here.

Chapter 3

HORTICULTURAL HISTORY

BULB IS ideally suited to surviving harsh and variable climates. Storing up food and energy in a secure underground cache, it can wait until times are favorable to flower. Tulips come from a land of severe climate, being native to Central Asia and the Pamir-Altai mountains. The daffodil or narcissus is native to the Mediterranean and the Middle East, as is the hyacinth. Both were known to the Greeks and are featured in myth and story. The iris is known in various forms throughout the temperate regions of the northern hemisphere and also figures prominently in Greek myth where Iris was the goddess of the rainbow.

Tulips were a relative latecomer to Europe. They were long cultivated by the Persians who called them *lalé*. Like the wild species these early varieties were unlike our common vase-shaped flowers, opening quickly to flat star shaped blossoms. They were also low growing and lacking the long season different varieties bring us today. The Turks obtained them from the Persians, and from distant parts of their own empire, like the Crimea. The Turks greatly admired them and even had a tulip blossom festival where the sultan selected an new favorite from his harem. In the 1550s Ogier Ghislain de Busbecq, the Austrian ambassador to Turkey, saw and described tulips in his letters home to Vienna. Busbecq brought tulips and tulip seeds home where they were propagated in the imperial gardens. He also gave them their name which he made out as *tulipam*, perhaps derived from *dulban*, or turban, in Turkish. This was not not a bad choice as the tight flower buds do look a bit like a turbaned head.

At this time Austria and Spain were both part of the Hapsburg domains, as were the Netherlands. Tulips were one of the beneficial effects of Spanish domination of Holland. The head of the imperial gardens in Vienna, Carolus Clusius, who later headed the medicinal gardens at the University of Leiden,

The early bloomer—Above: Red Emperor tulips with their almost metallic scarlet shading; Below: daffodils with forsythia behind them.

Bedded bulbs at Roosengaard, each in a large clump as they grow naturaly. Such thicker plantings carry much more visual impact than scatterings here and there.

Many of the species bulb varieties grow very unlike our garden standards. Tulips were originally small open stars like this rather than tight cups as now.

Above: The shimmering rows of tulip colors weave like a pastel textile: one of the reasons tulips are so successful in landscaping.
Right: From a slightly higher view other tulip fields turn into a bright checkerboard.

took tulips with him. Tulips thrived in the rich soil of Holland and within 50 years they were growing all over Holland. It was at this time that one of the most extraordinary stories of flowers took place. It is an instructive vision of human greed and folly, uniting elements of mass hysteria with telling satire of modern business "investment".

Although always popular as a new exotic, tulips suddenly became a consuming passion and toy of the rich. Under the influence of viral infection, tulips often "break" or produce sudden new color combinations. Since genetics and hybridizing were little understood this was one of the few ways of developing new varieties. Tulips began to sell for more and more money and by 1634 they were an investment item, often never changing hands when sold as in our futures market today. Special tulip markets were set up on the stock exchanges of major towns and special laws and regulations governing tulip sales were passed. Even the less wealthy indulged in the mania, forming clubs to buy and sell tulips.

The prices paid for unusual tulips such as *Viceroy* or *Semper Augustus* rose to incredible heights. For one *Viceroy* tulip it is reported that the following goods, valued at 2,500 florins, were paid: 2 loads of wheat, 4 loads of rye, 4 fat oxen, 8 fat pigs, 12 fat sheep, 2 hogsheads of wine, 4 barrels of 8-florin beer, 2 barrels of butter, 1,000 pounds of cheese, a complete bed, a suit of clothes and a silver beaker! Equally silly stories are told of the accidents of

fate. One hungry ship's captain, or in another version a sailor bringing good news to a tulip merchant, wanted an onion for his herrings. Spying a tulip and making a natural mistake he ate a 3,000 florin tulip for breakfast. He was lucky—tulips are highly edible. During the world wars the Dutch ate many of them to stay alive and healthy. Had the sailor eaten a daffodil he would have died at once.

As with all such get rich schemes it had to end sooner or later. Practical men felt the end coming and began adding escape clauses to their bills of sale. By late 1636 confidence in the value of tulips was weakening. Others started selling real tulips instead of only the rights of ownership on paper. Soon more and more entered the market. At last, on February 3, 1637 a buyer paid 1,000 florins for a bulb that had cost the seller 1,250. This ended tulip trade at that

market. Slowly, and then with sudden panic, the entire market for tulips collapsed and never rose again as it had been. Phony auctions to boost prices failed, and lawsuits flooded the courts as bankruptcy stuck thousands. It even threatened the financial stability of the country. The Court of Holland cancelled the obligations of unenforceable contracts and left sellers to settle as best they could, often for five to ten percent on the florin. It was years before trade in Holland fully recovered.

Interestingly, tulips were known in the new world before tulipmania struck, having come over on the *Mayflower*. The pilgrims spent some years in exile in Holland near Leiden, which was the earliest center of tulip growing. In America they were never tainted by the mania of wealth and have remained just a delightful spring flower.

The importance of your angle of view is easily seen in these two photographs. Above you can see how far apart the bulb rows are—one tractor wheel width.

When seen across the rows the fields suddenly appear solid.

Part of why the bulb fields show off so well is their early season of bloom. Most trees lack their leaves at this time and don't obscure the fields.

Daffodils, a common name for many of the narcissus family, have been known in Europe throughout history. Always a welcome harbinger of spring, they were never subject to such exotic fantasy as tulips. Their great antiquity is seen in the many names they have had—narcissus, porillon, daffy-down-dilly, fleur de coucou, lent lily and others. Daffodils are very enduring when planted and naturalize themselves readily. Their highly poisonous juices are partly why since animals will not eat them. So powerful are the toxins that flower pickers must wear gloves or risk serious skin problems. It is often recommended that you plant daffodils among your tulips to discourage mice who love to eat tulips. The toxins run for some distance through the soil on the daffodils roots. Like tulips they prefer rich and moist bottom soils as implied in the Greek myth of Narcissus.

Narcissus was a handsome but totally vain young man. He spent his time improving on his appearance and admiring himself. One day, when bending over a pool of still water so he could use it like a mirror, he fell in and drowned. Mourning the loss of such a beautiful creature, the gods turned him into the narcissus whose lovely blossoms nod over the waters next to which they so frequently grow. That he drowned at all is a demonstration of the firm belief in hubris which is found in Greek myth.

Hyacinths are found throughout Europe, although the large flowered varieties we most often grow descend from an oriental variety, *Hyacinthus Orientalis*. They too are long lasting and, like narcissus, poisonous. The best known European varieties are grape hyacinths and wild hyacinths, also known as scilla, wood hyacinths or bluebells. There is also an instructional Greek legend about hyacinths. Hyacinthus was a charming and handsome Spartan youth who was loved by both Apollo, the sun god, and Zephyrus, god of the west wind. Hyacinthus preferred Apollo and Zephyrus sought revenge for this slight. One day when Hyacinthus and Apollo we playing darts Zephyrus blew one astray and it killed Hyacinthus. Stricken with grief, Apollo made a purple flower from his blood and named it with the Greek word for sorrow—Hy (or *'ai* more properly). In more mundane and modern times, the juice of the hyacinth was used as a starch and glue. The ruffled collars of Elizabethan times often depended on hyacinth juice for their shape, and fletchers (arrowmakers) and bookbinders both found it the best of glues.

The iris was known throughout the ancient world, growing from Ireland to Siberia and as far south as North Africa. It was admired as a flower of beauty and imposing nobility. To the Greeks it was sacred to Hera, wife of Zeus and queen of the gods. In the Middle Ages the white iris became the symbol of the city of Florence and of the kings of France. Even today we associate the *fleur de lis* with France. Irises come in many forms and types. Most grow rhizomes, or creeping roots-stocks, at the surface of the ground. Others, like the Spanish Iris, grow from bulbs. It was these, brought to Holland by the Spanish Hapsburgs as the Austrians brought the tulip, that later became known as Dutch bulbous irises. Today they are the variety grown in the Skagit Valley—yellow, blue and white. Flowering last of all the bulbs in early May, they close out the season of mass bloom. To my thinking they are the most magnificent of all. Perhaps the fields are smaller and less overwhelming but the flowers are so much more complex and elegant. The smaller fields are more intimate and invite closer scrutiny, while the roads are no longer clogged with cars.

Hiding in leaves and grasses this escaped iris in a hedgerow still shows its delicate color and elegant form.

The Tulip Festival has a special collector's series poster every year. This concept was brought to the festival by Mount Vernon designer Galen Larson. Galen is also the designer of the festival logo, as well as the first annual poster shown to the right.

Each year the full color poster is distinctively different from its predecessors.

Galen Larson is currently working on a series of large botannical paintings of tulips that will be sold as prints, both at the festival and through galleries. The variety shown to the right is preludium.

Every year Kodak provides a special photographer's platform to facilitate the taking of shots from within the tulip fields. The balloon helps to locate the stand as well as advertise their film.

The aerial perspective provided by the platform gives photographers a different viewpoint.

Even the best of plans can't always make the weather cooperate. Tulips in the mist and rain are yet another experience for photographers. You have to be prepared for any kind of weather in the Northwest.

Display garden at Roosengaarde—one of the highlights of the Tulip festival. It seeks to create the feeling of an old Dutch garden.

Chapter 4

THE SKAGIT VALLEY TULIP FESTIVAL

*O*NCE BULBS BECAME A LARGE CROP in the Skagit Valley, the blooming fields of tulips suggested a festival. In 1946 the La Conner Civic Garden Club organized an annual Tulip Show where growers could display their best and the public enjoy them. This was the heyday of tulip growing in terms of number of growers. Over the years, the larger growers have thrived and the small ones disappeared. In 1956 the Washington State Bulb Commission had 30 members; in 1983 only 22. After a number of years the La Conner festival lost energy and the festival was taken over by Oak Harbor on Whidby Island. Other festivals continued, like the Daffodil Festival in Puyallup, but the Skagit's larger bulb growing area remained unknown to the public.

It was not until 1983 that various Chambers of Commerce of the Skagit Valley, looking for a promotional theme for tourism, decided to revive the festival. It was set up as a division of the Mount Vernon Chamber of Commerce, since Mount Vernon was the county seat and in a very central location. Participation and festival events are to be found in almost every town in the lower valley and it is a real unifying force on often isolated little towns. Together they do a much more impressive job than alone in competition. The festival was an immediate success, and now up to 200,000 people come each year to see the fields. Having been caught by accident in the traffic of the first festival, I can attest to the popularity of flowering fields. It took three hours to go six miles.

The choice of tulips as a theme was a good decision. Not only is there a certain romance about tulips, with their image of Holland's dikes and windmills, but they bloom at a more agreeable time of year than daffodils. I frequently attended the Puyallup Daffodil Festival as a child and remember it as a cold, gray, wet time of little pleasure. The weather is so variable in the

Mt. Baker in early spring, looking from Anacortes across Padilla Bay. Tillinghast Seed Company started on the south shore of Padilla Bay.

Northwest that early season crops are especially subject to widely variable blooming times. Some years the Puyallup festival had no flowers by festival time, other years they were long gone. Puyallup occasionally had the embarrassment of having to import daffodils from elsewhere in order to show some color. Tulips come late enough that no matter what the weather some will be in bloom. Visitors should be prepared for wind and rain as well as sun as both can occur, often in rapid succession. By way of example, 1988 was a cold and wet festival, while that of 1987 was warm and sunny.

The best times for flower viewing are during the week and in the mornings. Afternoons are always more crowded and the weekends are worst of all with frequent major traffic jams (otherwise unknown in the Skagit Valley). The Skagit Valley is just over an hour from either Seattle or Vancouver so it is easy to make spontaneous visits when weather or time are most fortuitous. It should be noted that during the festival many country roads have controlled traffic and one way travel. The map at the end of this book locates this year's growing fields and shows the requested direction of travel on all roads.

Even when picking tulips the job can be wet and cold, as in this 1988 photo. Although the pickers work hard they are well bundled up. The combination of clouds, shadow, sun and moisture of the Northwest spring make for dramatic coloration in the bulb fields.

Top: the bulbs do occasionally get a bit mixed up, but not always this obviously.
Above: the garden is laid out in formal Dutch beds.
Opposite: the authentic Dutch style windmill that is the centerpiece of the garden.

Each bed is heavily edged for a formal effect. Larger shrubs, such as rhododendrons, are planted in the center. This makes for an especially rich effect.

Mass blooming plants fill the beds for a carpet effect.

The tulips, on their long formal stems, rise above the ground cover.

Amid such masses of flowers, picking is the best reward.

The fields in the valley are the source of farmer's income and they should be respected as private. Even a small amount of casual trampling through them can cause serious financial loss. It is a privilege to be invited to enjoy the fields and every effort should be made to intrude as little as possible. Many of the valley inhabitants are less than enthusiastic about the crowds. When the festival started, there was a common bumper sticker that read "NUKE THE TULIPS", and many people are *still* unhappy about the hundreds of thousands of visitors. La Conner author Tom Robbins put it well when he noted that he loved the tulips and felt it was nice that people wanted to plant and enjoy them. Yet, he finds it hard to accept a tulip "industry", feeling that "the wonders of nature are not just something to be exploited for money". We should not let our enjoyment of the flowers make others dislike and regret them.

There are three display gardens for viewing and purchasing numerous varieties of bulbs and flowers (bulbs are shipped in the fall). **Westshore Acres** at 956 Downey Road (at the west end of McLean road) is the longest established. They are growers of the bulbs they display and sell. **Roozengaarde** is the display garden of Washington Bulb Company at 1587 Beaver Marsh road. It is laid out like a Dutch garden, complete with windmill. **La Conner Flats** is a new display garden established by Hart's Nursery at 1598 Best Road. It is heavily planted in a wide variety of plants and is in a state of showy display most of the year. In addition to the adjacent nursery there is a restaurant on the premises. Although not elaborate enough to compete with famous sites like Buchart Gardens, it is a popular year-round destination for thousands of visitors.

*Special decorations are
made for the festival.*

SPECIAL FESTIVAL EVENTS

One of the most charming festival events is the chosing of "Little Miss Tulip" for the year.

The food concessions try to show distinctive local 'flavors'. This one displays a little black humor while reminding us of the large settlement of North Carolina "Tarheels" in the upper valley.

Community fairs and parades give local residents a chance to share the festival activities with visitors. In the foreground you can see one of the many antique cars that take part in the antique car show and cruise.

Besides viewing the flower fields the following events are also part of the festival for 1989:

April 1–16	**Cleave's Greenhouse U-pick Tulip Field**—Mt. Vernon on old hwy. 99
Weekends,	**Pacific NW Schooner Cruise**—Anacortes, 11 A.M., 2 & 5 P.M. at Cap Sante Boat Haven
April 1	**10K Run & Annual Slug Run**—Burlington at I-5 exit 229, 10 A.M.
April 6	**Robert Ruth Art Show Opening**—Galley 5 restaurant in Burlington
April 7–9	Downtown Mt. Vernon Street Fair
April 7	**Tulip Festival Quilt Show**—Sedro Woolley Senior Center, 820 State St.
April 8	**Mt. Vernon Christian School Pancake Breakfast**—820 Blackburn St. 7 A.M.–1 P.M.
"	**PAACCAR Technical Center Open House**—Hwy. 237, one mile north of hwy. 20
"	**Guitanna Memorial Tulip Festival Gymnastics Meet**—Mt. Vernon, 309 Milwaukee St., 10 A.M. & 2 P.M.
"	**Sock Hop For Over 21 Crowd**—Mt. Vernon, Skagit Valley Mall, 8–12 P.M.
"	**Silent Movies at the Lincoln**—Mt. Vernon, 712 South 1st, 12–4 P.M.
April 8–9	**Vela Luka Croatian Dance**—Mt. Vernon, Lincoln Theatre, 712 S. 1st, 7:30 P.M. April 8, 3 P.M. April 9
"	**Mt. Vernon Kiwanis Salmon Barbeque**—Hillcrest Park in Mt. Vernon, 11 A.M.–5 P.M.
April 14–16	**"A Taste of Skagit" Food Fair**—Downtown Anacortes. Food, beer, wine and numerous events.
April 15–16	**Kiwanis Salmon Barbeque**—Hillcrest Park in Mt. Vernon, 11 A.M.–4 P.M.
April 15	**Domino's Pizza/Anacortes Yacht Club Regatta**—Anacortes, in Padilla Bay. Spectators use Cap Sante Hill.
"	**Skagit Valley Tulip Festival Car Show**—Anacortes, 10th & Commercial
"	**Sousa & His Band Concert**—Mt. Vernon at the Lincoln Theatre, 712 S. 1st, 7:30 P.M.

April 16	**"Tulip Pedal" Bicycle Ride**— Start in Edgewater Park Mt. Vernon, 9 A.M.–3 P.M.
"	**J.J.'s Car Show & Tulip Cruise**—Special interest & vintage cars cruise the fields with stops in Anacortes, Burlington, La Conner & Mt. Vernon
"	**Sousa & His Band Concert**—Anacortes, Brodniak Hall at Anacortes High School, 19th & J St, 3 P.M.

Chapter 5
OTHER PLEASURES

THERE ARE MANY THINGS TO DO in the Skagit Valley besides look at flowers. Some of the most interesting center around its still numerous wilderness areas and wildlife. The county has only 70,000 inhabitants, and the bulk of it is forest and mountains. Like so many Puget Sound areas the terrain ranges from seashore to the high mountains of the North Cascades.

The mountains include access to the Skagit dams of Seattle City Light and the Ross Lake recreation area, the North Cascade Pass Highway to the Methow Valley, and the Cascade Pass trail system. These areas receive high rainfall and lie deep in snow during the winter, but are excellent summer hiking country. The passes are quite high and sudden changes in weather should be prepared for. The many rivers that run out of the mountains are popular whitewater sites, but experience is especially important on these rapidly flowing rivers.

Skagit County has excellent salt water access that is open year round. Deception Pass State Park has all kinds of beaches as well as lowland forest. Nearby is Mt. Erie Park with spectacular views of the entire region. At the northern edge of the county along Chuckanut Drive is Larrabee State Park with thousands of feet of beach and 1,886 acres of hills and forest.

The best known inhabitants and visitors of Skagit County may well be the numerous species of birds found there. In addition to the many year round species, large numbers of ducks, geese, swans, and bald eagles are seasonal visitors. The eagles are most commonly seen on the upper Skagit, where migrating salmon pile up on the rocks near Rockport. Howard Miller Steelhead Park and Eagle View Park are good areas to visit. Numerous tours are run for those seeking a guided experience. Eagles are seen throughout the

Top left: *A soaring bald eagle. The eagles are primarily fish feeders and come in large numbers to follow the spawning salmon.*
Top right: *An old water tower, often the only survivor of an early homestead. Swallows gather here by day, and bats by night.*
Bottom: *Feeding swans in the wet winter farmland. To them this is the perfect environment for a southern vacation from their frozen breeding grounds.*

Sunset over Similk Bay. Skagit County has a long coastline cut by many bays and rivers, and the protected waters permit year round boating.

Swans practice landing in a farmer's field. The large birds feed heavily before returning north to breed. Their annual departure is sudden and somehow related to their sensing of the necessary change in the weather thousands of miles away in the Arctic ocean.

county, however. At my house at the Skagit's mouth, I have had eagles fly by only 10 feet from my balcony.

In the lowland areas it is the coast that has the most noteworthy sites, although I have seen flocks of trumpeter swans floating over fields like flying sheep. The Brezeale-Padilla Bay National Estuarine Research Reserve and Interpretive Center, located near Bay View on Padilla Bay, is a marvelous place to visit. It is one of the finest sites for wetland birds in the country. To the south, on Fir Island, is the Skagit Wildlife Recreational Area. Heavily used by duck and goose hunters in the fall, it is well populated with numerous waterfowl and is good for bird watching at other times. Each season has its characteristic species and is a rewarding time for observation. My own lists contain over 100 varieties and are still growing. Using a boat or kayak is of much help to quietly move through the bird's watery domain. Many launching sites are found in the county.

Above: Hikers in the North Cascades. Skagit County is a major access route to this imposing wilderness.
Below: The rugged Cascades offer a constantly changing series of vistas and settings for those willing to do some serious walking.

Top: Kayaker on the Sauk River. The heavy rainfall and sudden descent of Skagit County rivers makes for excellent white water boating.
Bottom: For those interested in less strenuous activity there are many gently wooded trails.

Chapter 6
PLACES TO STAY & EAT

THE SKAGIT VALLEY is a popular vacation destination and there are a growing number of delightful inns and restaurants to tempt you. It is a quiet and restful place to visit, especially in the summer. Visitors often come from Vancouver, B.C. or Seattle just for dinner in one of the attractive waterfront restaurants, and perhaps a quiet night away from home. At last count there were 26 motels and hotels and 19 bed and breakfast establishments in the county. Most of them are in the lower valley and are conveniently near the tulip fields. The following selection isn't complete but it lists those I know something about.

La Conner—*Victorian romance revived*

Downey House
1880 Chilberg Road   466–3207
A quiet country bed & breakfast with views, hot tub and antique furnished rooms. Good breakfasts and pies worth remembering with two wonderful hosts. A few miles east of town.

Heather House
505 Maple   466–4675
A replica of an 1890 Cape Cod home with spectacular views. Run by a 'make yourself at home' method, visitors are given freedom to relax and raid the ice box if they wish.

The Heron
117 Maple   466–4626
Located at the entrance to La Conner, this new hotel has antique charm
and a view of the valley and mountains. Whirlpool and private baths.
Reservation deposit required.

Katy's Inn
Third & Washington   466–3366
Originally built in 1876 as Capt. John Peck's home, this small bed &
breakfast is furnished with antiques to recapture that past. Each guest
room has a balcony view of La Conner and the Swinomish Slough.
Refreshments during the day as well as breakfast.

La Conner Country Inn
Second & Morris Street   466–3101
A completely new building that is in character with La Conner's Victorian
past. It is immensely popular, with a fireplace in every room and complimentary breakfast in the parlour. Even though it is the largest in the area,
reservations are suggested.

Rainbow Inn
1075 Chilberg Road   466–4578
A much elaborated farm house one mile east of La Conner. Antique decor,
queen size beds, hot tub and fireplace, but not all have private baths. Pets
can be accommodated. Their breakfasts are a hearty start to the day.

Raymond House
604 Second St.   466–3417
Waterfront views one block above the heart of town.

White Swan Guest House
1388 Moore Road   445–6805
Located about six miles from La Conner on Fir Island. Only three guest
rooms in the quiet farm house for a very private bed & breakfast. Fir Island
is still real farmland untouched by tourism.

Potlatch RV Resort
End of Third St.   466–4468
If you want to bring your RV this is your place. Pool, hot tub and
laundromat are available here. Reservations requested.

RESTAURANTS

Barkley's of La Conner
In the La Conner Country Inn   466–4261
Well known and with a good menu.

The Black Swan
505 S. First St.   466–3040
A magnificent restaurant worth a visit on its own. I often drive up from
Seattle for lunch. The only complaint is that it is so small that reservations
are usually essential.

Café Pojanté
612 S. First St. (On the balcony of Skagit Bay Books)
Espresso with a view and culture.

The Calico Cupboard
720 S. First St.   466–4451
A bakery and cafe that serves first class breakfasts and lunches. A courtyard
can be used in warm weather. Take something home with you from the
bakery—I usually do.

Farmhouse Inn
Highway 20 at La Conner-Whitney Road   466–4411
Hearty and reasonable country dining in a pleasant atmosphere. This is
where many of the local families eat along with millions of tourists. The
swedish meatballs, corn bread and pies are special.

La Conner Seafood & Prime Rib House
614 First St.   466–4014
After many identities this noted tavern site seems to have found one that
works. Good food and a relaxing atmosphere.

57

Red emperor tulips are very popular for their early and large bright red blooms. The bloom time of red emperors is a safe time for starting gardens since it indicates warmer ground.

Roosengaard is not the only nursery to decorate for the festival. The Skagit Valley Bulb Farm is another major grower.

Daffodils are an entirely different world of color. Their brilliant single color can stain the whole atmosphere. This is especially true in the golden light of sunset, as in this photograph.

The time of year changes the quality of Skagit light over a wide range.
Above: In midsummer the strong sunlight paints the river like a pastel Monet painting.
Below: Bright sunlight on daffodils creates an almost surreal field. You shouldn't be too surprised if Dorothy and Toto stepped out of them.

The Lighthouse Inn
512 S. First St.   466–3147
Fine seafood in La Conner's best known restaurant. The waterfront views
match the food. There is a deli sandwich shop on the front for quicker
meals.

Mt. Vernon—*On the freeway and back to the 20th century*

Best Western Motor Inn
300 W. College Way   424–4287
Good quality rooms. Pool and whirlpool available. Many rooms with
refrigerators or radios. AAA listed.

Chuckanut Manor
S. end of Chuckanut Drive   766–6191
Off by itself, it is hard to decide where to place this classic and famous bed
& breakfast-restaurant combination. You'll see it again under restaurants.
Fabulous view.

Mount Vernon Travelodge
1910 freeway Drive   428–7020
High season rates start with the Tulip Festival here, but the rooms are
comfortable. Bridal Suite (if you want to plan ahead), indoor pool, jacuzzi,
exercise room and coin laundry are available. AAA listed.

Nendel's Motor Inn
2009 Riverside Drive   424–4141
The largest motel in the valley with lots of extras—king and queen size
beds, executive suites with wet bars, etc. Heated pool, health club privi-
leges and complimentary breakfasts for the rest of us. AAA listed.

Sterling Motor Inn
866 S. Garl (Burlington)   757–0051
Located just north of Mt. Vernon at the Highway 20 exit. Movies, radios,
phones and pets being permitted are some of its features. A better than
average restaurant is adjacent and open Tuesday–Sunday from 6 a.m. AAA
listed. Reservation deposit is required.

Smith House Bed & Breakfast
307 Maple St. (Hamilton)   826–4214
Located some 16 miles east of Burlington off Highway 20 this one is on
the edge of the tulip area, but too nice to leave out. In a restored 1909
farmhouse the five bedrooms are furnished with antiques. Breakfast is
solid, good and a fitting end to an old fashioned stay.

Clarks Skagit River Cabins & Eatery
5675 N. Cascade Highway 20 (Rockport)   873–2250
Even more afield is this Skagit classic. Basic but comfortable, and most
convenient for eagle watching and its edge of the wilderness location. RV
and tent camping allowed. Lots of rural extras.

RESTAURANTS

The Granary
1598 Best Road   466–3821
Adjacent to Skagit Flats display gardens. A convenient refueling stop after
wandering among the flowers.

Knotty Pine Cafe
521 S. Second   336–5061
A reasonably priced family restaurant that has been there forever, or so it
seems. Valley people come here.

The Longfellow
120 N. First   336–3684
A Mt. Vernon expansion by the people who do the Rhododendron.
Another magnificent restaurant that could hold its own anywhere. The
best of local products.

Mexico Cafe
1590 Memorial Highway   424–1977
Many hispanics have settled in the Skagit valley to work the farmland, and
so you will find an unusual concentration of Mexican restaurants for such
a small population. Everyone has their favorite and this is mine. The food
is distinctive and tasty and I especially recommend the chile rellenos.

The region is very similar to Norway, but with a much milder climate. Above: A church beneath Mt. Baker. Below: The mouth of the Skagit. Ika Island, in the middle distance, is the second in a long line of rocky islands that stretch through the San Juans north past Vancouver Island. All the islands of the south Sound are sandy islands.

Left: The Vela Luka dancers are a legacy of the large settlement of Yugoslavian fishermen in Anacortes. Below: Sailboats near Anacortes.

Above: Wheat field and an old barn. Right: Picked tulips brighten any spot. The tight bud at the upper right is at the correct picking stage for cut flowers.

The Monkey Business Cafe
309 Pine St.   336–5212
Proof that good quality can work, this deli has been around for a long time.
I always enjoy stopping in for restorative food after a hike through the
fields and woods.

The Rhododendron Cafe
533 Chuckanut Drive (Bow)   766–6667
Saving the best for last lets me dream on about another great restaurant
worth a trip for a meal. Originally only a diner at a crossroads, this has
become one of the Northwest's finest in the hands of sensitive owners.

Anacortes—*Edge of the San Juans & a world to itself*

Alice Bay Bed & Breakfast
982 Scott Road (Bow)   766–6396
In the country on the south side of Samish Island, some 10 miles from
Anacortes (or Mt. Vernon or La Conner for that matter), west of the
entrance to Chuckanut Drive. It is quiet and delightfully eccentric.
Futons, private baths, sauna and hot tub and a continental breakfast
highlight this non-smoking inn.

Campbell House
36th & Commercial   293–4910
A bed & breakfast in a historic home. Full breakfast and a welcome to
children highlight their service.

Dutch Treat House
31st & M Ave.   293–8154
Large rooms and full breakfast in an old Dutch style home.

Hasty Pudding House
1312 – 8th St.   293–5773
I quite honestly don't know anything about this bed & breakfast, but with
a name like that I'd stay there just to find out.

Islands Motel
3401 Commercial   293–4644

Of the four AAA rated motels in Anacortes this is my favorite. Landscaping and beautiful views go well with first class rooms. Many rooms have fireplaces or refrigerators, and there is a heated pool and whirlpool. The adjacent restaurant, La Petite, is another plus. Reservation deposit required.

Nantucket Inn
3402 Commercial Ave.   293–6007
A famous and fine bed & breakfast run by a marvelous quilter. It is furnished with antiques and, surprise, quilts on the beds. Some quilts are for sale. There is a fireplace, but no smoking or pets.

Old Brook Inn
530 Old brook Lane   293–4768
The ultimate in private rural tranquility. Continental breakfast where you can pick your own berries in season. *The* bedroom is on the first floor with a great view.

RESTAURANTS

Boomers Landing
209 T St.   293–5108
Overlooking Guemes Channel, Boomers has excellent seafood (& other choices) with a view to match.

Chuckanut Manor
S. end of Chuckanut Drive   766–6191
Everything from champagne brunch to seafood and steaks. A good choice of food and a first class view. You can stay here, too.

La Petite
3401 Commercial   293–4644
First class dining with a Danish touch.

Although more subtle than some, the Northwest autumn can show much color.
Above: Vine maples spill down the hillside.
Below: In years of long, dry autumns the leaves can take on unusual shades due to changes in trapped sugars.

"Tulips are beautiful but they are impossible to render. When I saw them I said to myself that they could not be painted. ...I love them, and when the flowers are in bloom, are picked and piled all at once on the little canals, they form rafts of color...on the blue reflection of the sky."
Claude Monet

Chapter 7

WHERE TO BUY BULBS & PLANTS

HE SKAGIT VALLEY has long been a productive source of nursery stock for sale throughout the country. Rhododendrons, perennials and shrubs have been grown here longer than bulbs and thrive in the moist and mild Northwest climate. Some of the growers are wholesale only, but a large number sell garden bulbs and plants at retail. Among the nurseries you might try:

Cleave's Greenhouse
1709 Old Highway 99 (Mt. Vernon)   424–1155
Annuals, perennials, potted plants and a u-pick tulip field.

Hart's Nursery
1578 Best Road   466–3821
Associated with Skagit Flats display gardens this is one of the largest nurseries in the valley. There is a fee to tour the display gardens.

Roosengaarde
1587 Beaver Marsh Road   424–8531
Display garden for bulbs and sales of flowers in season. Associated with the Washington Bulb Company (next door). Bulbs can be ordered for seasonal delivery.

Skagit Valley Gardens
1695 Johnson Road   424–6760
Located on the west frontage road north of Conway they have a good selection of shrubs, trees and plants.

Skagit Valley Bulb Farm
1502 Bradshaw Road   424–8152
Walk-in fields with cut flower and bulb sales.

Summersun Greenhouse
4100 E. College Way (Mt. Vernon)   424–1663
An extensive selection of plants.

Tillinghast Seed Company
617 E. Morris (La Conner)   466–3329
A little bit of everything and a lot of most. The original nursery and seed
company in the Northwest.

Wells Nursery
424 E. Section St. (Mt. Vernon)   336–6544
An especially good selection of shrubs and trees. Located on the east side
of the freeway in south Mt. Vernon.

West Shore Acres
956 Downey Road   466–3158
Located at the west end of McLean Road along the Swinomish Slough.
They provide good access to tulip fields and sell flowers and bulbs.

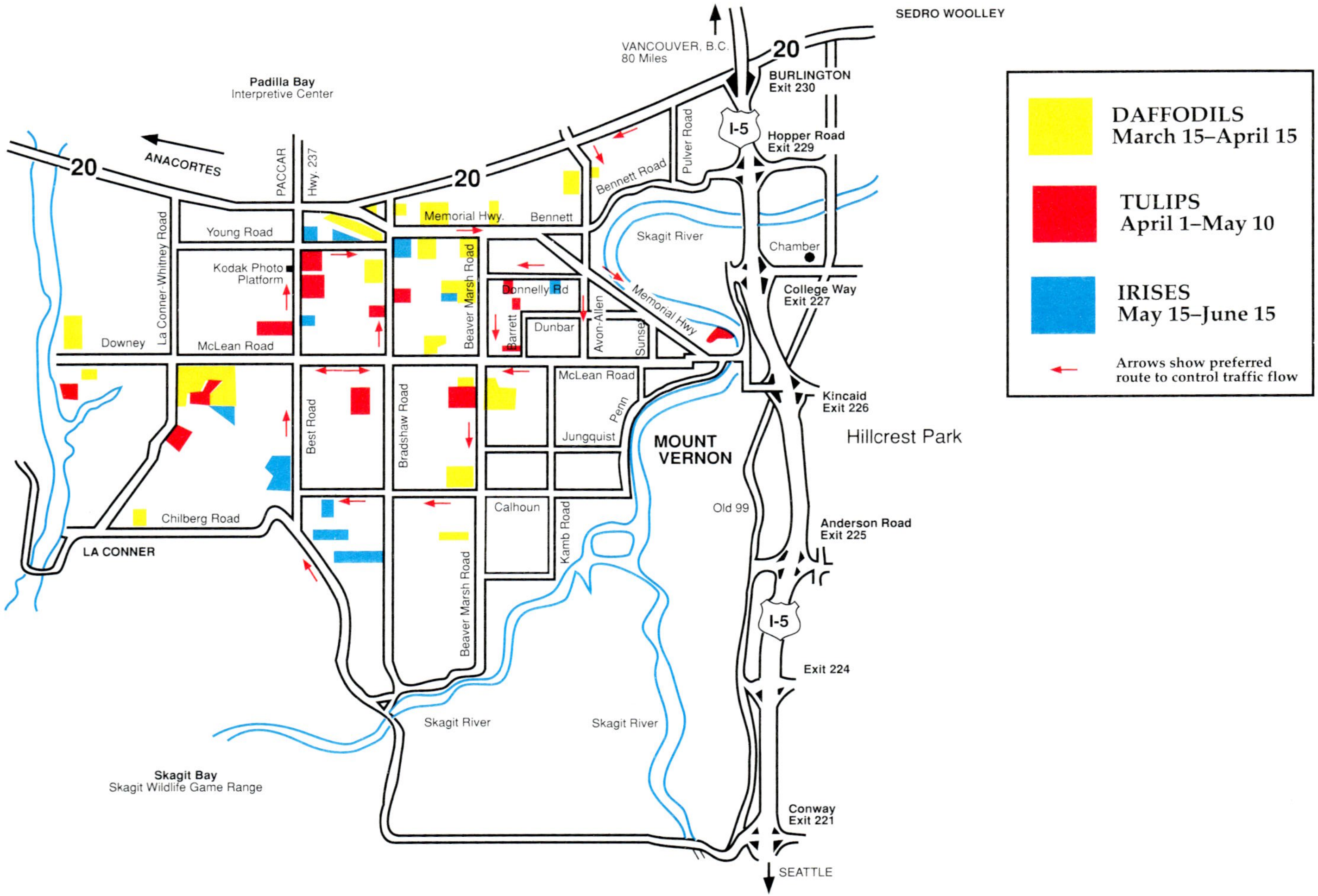

DAFFODILS
March 15–April 15

TULIPS
April 1–May 10

IRISES
May 15–June 15

Arrows show preferred route to control traffic flow

SEDRO WOOLLEY

VANCOUVER, B.C.
80 Miles

20

BURLINGTON
Exit 230

I-5

Hopper Road
Exit 229

Pulver Road

Bennett Road

Skagit River

Chamber

College Way
Exit 227

Memorial Hwy

Padilla Bay
Interpretive Center

ANACORTES

20

PACCAR

Hwy. 237

Memorial Hwy.

Bennett

Young Road

La Conner-Whitney Road

Kodak Photo Platform

Downey

McLean Road

Donnelly Rd

Dunbar

Barrett

Avon-Allen

Sunset

Beaver Marsh Road

McLean Road

Kincaid
Exit 226

Hillcrest Park

MOUNT VERNON

Best Road

Bradshaw Road

Penn

Jungquist

Calhoun

Kamb Road

Old 99

Anderson Road
Exit 225

I-5

Exit 224

LA CONNER

Chilberg Road

Skagit River

Skagit River

Conway
Exit 221

SEATTLE

Skagit Bay
Skagit Wildlife Game Range